RUBANK EDUCATIONAL LIBRARY No. 105

RUBANK

Advanced Method

BASSOON

Vol. I

H. VOXMAN
AND
WM. GOWER

AN OUTLINED COURSE OF STUDY
DESIGNED TO FOLLOW UP ANY
OF THE VARIOUS ELEMENTARY
AND INTERMEDIATE METHODS

RUBANK®

HAL•LEONARD®
CORPORATION
7777 W. BLUEMOUND RD. P.O. BOX 13819 MILWAUKEE, WI 53213

NOTE

THE RUBANK ADVANCED METHOD for Bassoon is published in two volumes, the course of study being divided in the following manner:

Vol. I
- Keys of C, F, G, B♭, and D Major.
- Keys of A, D, E, G, and B Minor.

Vol. II
- Keys of E♭, A, A♭, E, D♭, and B Major.
- Keys of C, F♯, F, and C♯ Minor.

PREFACE

THIS METHOD is designed to follow any of the various Elementary and Intermediate instruction series, or Elementary instruction series comprising two or more volumes, depending upon the previous development of the student. The authors have found it necessary in their teaching experience to draw from many sources in order to provide a progressive course of study. The present publication assembles in two volumes, the material essential to a well-rounded musical development.

THE OUTLINES, one of which is included in each of the respective volumes, tend to afford an objective picture of the student's progress. They will facilitate the ranking of members in a large ensemble or they may serve as a basis for awards of merit. In addition, a one-sided development along strictly technical or strictly melodic lines is avoided. The use of these outlines, however, is not imperative and they may be discarded at the discretion of the teacher.

H. Voxman — Wm. Gower

OUTLINE
OF
RUBANK ADVANCED METHOD
FOR
BASSOON, Vol. I
BY
H. Voxman and Wm. Gower

UNIT	SCALES and ARPEGGIOS (Key)			MELODIC INTERPRE-TATION	ARTICU-LATION	FINGER EXERCISES	ORNA-MENTS	SOLOS	UNIT COM-PLETED
1	5 (1) 6 (5)		C	19 (1) (1a)	41 (1)	54 (1) (2)	60 (1)	69 (1)	
2	5 (2) 6 (6)		C	20 (2) (2a)	41 (2)	54 (3) (4)	60 (2)	69 (1)	
3	5 (3) 6 (7)		C	20 (3) 21 (3a)	42 (3)	54 (5) (6)	60 (3)	69 (1)	
4	6 (4) 6 (8)		C	21 (4) (4a)	42 (4)	54 (7) (8)	60 (4)	69 (1)	
5	6 (9)		a	22 (5)	43 (5)	54 (9) (10)	60 (5)	69 (1)	
6	6 (10) 7 (13)		a	23 (6)	43 (6)	54 (11) (12)	61 (6)	69 (1)	
7	7 (11) (14)		a	23 (7)	43 (7)	54 (13) (14)	61 (7)	69 (2)	
8	7 (12) (15) (16)		a	23 (8)	43 (7)	54 (15) (16) (17)	61 (7)	69 (2)	
9	8 (17) 9 (21)		F	24 (9)	44 (8)	54 (18) (19)	62 (8) (9)	69 (2)	
10	8 (18) 9 (22)		F	25 (10)	44 (9)	54 (20) (21)	62 (10)	69 (2)	
11	8 (19) 9 (23)		F	26 (11)	44 (10)	54 (22) (23)	62 (10)	69 (2)	
12	9 (20) (24)		F	26 (11)	44 (10)	54 (24) (25)	63 (11) (12)	69 (2)	
13	10 (25)		d	27 (12)	45 (11)	54 (26) (27)	63 (13) (14)	70 (3)	
14	10 (26) (28)		d	27 (13)	45 (12)	54 (28) (29)	63 (15) (16)	70 (3)	
15	10 (27) (29) (30)		d	27 (13)	45 (12)	54 (30) (31) (32)	64 (17) (18) (19)	70 (3)	
16	11 (31) 12 (35)		G	28 (14)	46 (13)	54 (33) (34)	64 (20)	70 (3)	
17	11 (32) 12 (36)		G	28 (14)	46 (14)	54 (35) (36) (37)	64 (20)	70 (3)	
18	11 (33) 12 (37)		G	30 (15)	46 (15)	54 (38) (39) (40)	65 (21) (22)	70 (3)	
19	11 (34) 12 (38)		G	31 (16)	46 (15)	55 (41) (42)	65 (23)	70 (4)	
20	12 (39)		e	31 (17)	47 (16)	55 (43) (44)	65 (24)	70 (4)	
21	12 (40) 13 (42) (43)		e	31 (17)	47 (17)	55 (45) (46)	65 (25)	70 (4)	
22	13 (41) (44) (45)		e	31 (17)	48 (18)	55 (47) (48)	65 (26)	70 (4)	
23	14 (46) 15 (50)		Bb	32 (18)	48 (19)	55 (49) (50)	65 (27)	70 (4)	
24	14 (47) 15 (51)		Bb	33 (19)	48 (20)	55 (51) (52)	66 (28)	70 (4)	
25	14 (48) 15 (52)		Bb	33 (20)	49 (21)	55 (53) (54)	66 (29) (30)	71 (5)	
26	14 (49) 15 (53)		Bb	33 (20)	49 (22)	55 (55) (56)	67 (31)	71 (5)	
27	15 (54)		g	36 (21)	50 (23)	55 (57) (58)	67 (31)	71 (5)	
28	15 (55) 16 (57)		g	36 (22)	50 (24)	55 (59) (60)	67 (32)	71 (5)	
29	16 (56) (58) (59)		g	37 (23)	50 (24)	55 (61) (62) (63)	67 (32)	71 (5)	
30	16 (60) 17 (64)		D	38 (24)	51 (25)	55 (64) (65)	67 (33)	71 (5)	
31	17 (61) 18 (65)		D	38 (25)	51 (26)	55 (66) (67) (68)	67 (34)	72 (6)	
32	17 (62) 18 (66)		D	38 (25)	52 (27)	55 (69) (70)	67 (35)	72 (6)	
33	17 (63)		D	39 (26)	52 (27)	55 (71) (72) (73)	68 (36)	72 (6)	
34	18 (67)		b	39 (27)	53 (28)	55 (74) (75)	68 (36)	72 (6)	
35	18 (68) (70)		b	40 (28)	53 (29)	55 (76) (77)	68 (36)	72 (6)	
36	18 (69) (71) (72)		b	40 (28)	53 (30)	55 (78) (79) (80)	68 (36)	72 (6)	

NUMERALS designate page number.
ENCIRCLED NUMBERS designate exercise number.
COMPLETED EXERCISES may be indicated by crossing out the rings, thus, ⊗.

889-68

PRACTICE AND GRADE REPORT

SECOND SEMESTER

Student's Name _____ Date _____

Week	Sun.	Mon.	Tue.	Wed.	Thu.	Fri.	Sat.	Total	Parent's Signature	Grade
1										
2										
3										
4										
5										
6										
7										
8										
9										
10										
11										
12										
13										
14										
15										
16										
17										
18										
19										
20										

Semester Grade _____

Instructor's Signature _____

FIRST SEMESTER

Student's Name _____ Date _____

Week	Sun.	Mon.	Tue.	Wed.	Thu.	Fri.	Sat.	Total	Parent's Signature	Grade
1										
2										
3										
4										
5										
6										
7										
8										
9										
10										
11										
12										
13										
14										
15										
16										
17										
18										
19										
20										

Semester Grade _____

Instructor's Signature _____

Scales and Arpeggios

C Major

© Copyright MCMXLII by Rubank, Inc., Chicago, Ill.
International Copyright Secured

Various articulations may be used in the chromatic, the interval, and the arpeggio exercises at the option of the instructor.

Chromatic Scale

Exercise in Thirds

Common Chord

Dominant 7th Chord

A Minor

The sign ⌢ indicates a half step

Original

Harmonic

Melodic

Exercise in Thirds

Common Chord

Diminished 7th Chord

F Major

20

simile

21

Exercise in Thirds

22

Common Chord

23

Dominant 7th Chord

24

D Minor

Original **Harmonic**

25

Melodic

26

27

Thirds

28

Common Chord

29

Diminished 7th Chord

30

G Major

31

32

simile

simile

33

34

35

Thirds

36

Common Chord

37

Dominant 7th Chord

38

E Minor

Original   **Harmonic**

39

Melodic

40

simile

simile

41

simile

42

Thirds

43

Common Chord

44

Diminished 7th Chord

45

B♭ Major

Practice also an octave lower

etc.

simile

50

Thirds
8va ad lib.

51

Common Chord

52

Dominant 7th Chord

53

G Minor

Original   **Harmonic**

54

Melodic

55

simile

simile

Thirds

Common Chord

Diminished 7th Chord

D Major

61

62

simile

63

Thirds

64

Common Chord

65

Dominant 7th Chord

66

B Minor

Original   **Harmonic**

67

Melodic

68

69

simile

Thirds
8va ad lib.

70

Common Chord

71

Diminished 7th Chord

72

Studies in Melodic Interpretation

For One or Two Part Playing

The following studies are designed to aid in the development of the student's interpretative ability. Careful attention to the marks of expression is essential to effective use of the material. Pencil the technically difficult passages and devote extra time to their mastery.

In rhythmic music in the more rapid tempi (marches, dances, etc.) tones that are equal divisions of the beat are played somewhat detached (staccato). Tones that equal a beat or are multiples of a beat are held full value. Tones followed by rests are usually held full value. This point should be especially observed in slow music.

HOHMANN

Tenor Clef

To avoid an excessive use of the leger lines above the staff, music for the bassoon is frequently written in the Tenor clef, 𝄡. This clef indicates that middle C is found on the fourth line of the staff. For this reason it is frequently called the C-clef.

20

BERR

Moderato

Old Hundredth

JANCOURT

Andante

Lento

889-68

3a
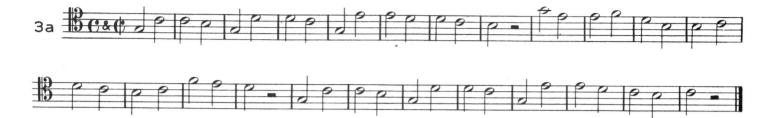

Andante con moto

4

WEISSENBORN

4a

889-68

Allegro moderato

WEISSENBORN

6

Allegro poco agitato

JANCOURT

7

Andante

WEISSENBORN

8

OZI

Allegro moderato

9

Allegretto

10

Allegretto

11

WEISSENBORN

SLAMA

DOTZAUER

Allegretto

14

Var. I

Var. II

Var. III

Moderato

15

16 Andantino — JANCOURT

p con espressivo

rall. *p a tempo*

17 Lento — LEFÈVRE

D.C. al Fine

DOTZAUER

Andante

18

JANCOURT

19

OZI

20

Var. I

Var. II

Var. III

HOHMANN

21

JANCOURT

22

MAZAS

Moderato

23

DOTZAUER

24

WEISSENBORN

25

Leggiero e semplice

LEFÈVRE

26

OZI

Poco presto

27

JANCOURT

Studies in Articulation

In all exercises where no tempo is indicated, the student should play the study as rapidly as is consistent with tonal control and technical accuracy. The first practice on each exercise should be done very slowly in order that the articulation may be carefully observed.

In allegro tempi figures similar to 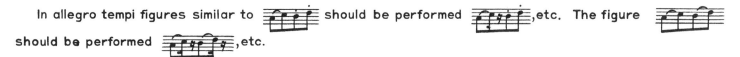 should be performed ,etc. The figure should be performed ,etc.

The material for this section is taken from the works of Weissenborn, Jancourt, Ozi, etc.

Moderato

Moderato

Allegro moderato

3

Fine

D.C. al Fine

Allegro moderato

4

Moderato

8

Moderato

9

Allegretto

10

D. C. al Fine

11

Poco lento

12

mf

pesante   ritard.

889-68

13

Allegro

14

Fine

D. C. al Fine

15

mf

Andante

21

Andante con moto

22

Marcia

risoluto

23

poco forte

sf   *sf*   *p dolce*

cresc.   *f*

sf   *sf*

Andante con moto

24

delicately, but with expression

Moderato

25

dolce

Fine

D.C. al Fine

26

simile

Allegretto

TRIO

Andante

dolce

fz

Allegro

Exercises in Fingering

Practice these exercises slowly and increase in rapidity as the difficulties in fingering are overcome.

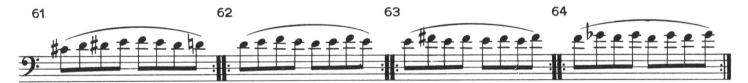

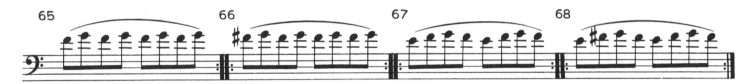

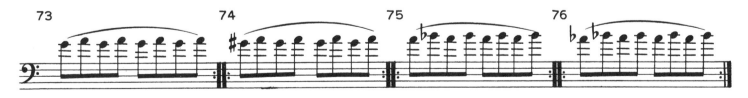

Table of Trills for Bassoon (Heckel System)

1. Low Bb Key
2. Low B "
3. Low C "
4. Low D "
5. High C "
6. High A "
7. C# "
8. Bb "
9. Low E "
10. F# "
11. G#-Ab "
12. G#-Ab "
13. Low F "
14. F# "
15. G "
16. Bb "
17. C# "
18. Low C# "
19. Low Eb "
R. Vent "

For this trill	play	trill	with	of the
	C	low C# key (18)	4th finger	left hand
	D	Eb key (19)	4th finger	l.h.
	D	D key (4)	thumb	l.h.
	Eb	D key (4)	thumb	l.h.
	Eb	thumb of the left hand and thumb of the right hand simultaneously.		
	E	E key (9)	thumb	right hand
	E	F key (13)	4th finger	r.h.
	F	F# key (10)	thumb	r.h.
	F	F key (13)	4th finger	r.h.
	F# (key 10) or F# (key 14)	F# key (10) / F# key (14)	thumb / 4th finger	r.h. / r.h.
	F# (key 10) or F# (key 14)	G# key (12) / G# key (11)	4th finger / thumb	r.h. / r.h.
	G	G# key 12 or 11	4th finger or thumb	r.h. / r.h.
	G	G key (15)	3rd finger	r.h.
	G# with key 12 or 11	G key (15)	3rd finger	r.h.
	Ab with key 12	Bb key (8)	thumb	r.h.
	A	Bb key 16 or 8	3rd finger or thumb	r.h. / r.h.
	A		2nd finger	r.h.

For this trill	play	trill	with	of the	Remarks
(notation)	Bb with key 16 or key 8		2nd finger	r.h.	
(notation)	Bb with key 16 or key 8		1st & 2nd fingers	r.h.	
(notation)	B		1st finger	r.h.	
(notation)	B		3rd finger	l.h.	
(notation)	C	C# key 7 or 17	thumb or 1st finger	l.h. r.h.	
(notation)	C		3rd finger	l.h.	
(notation)	C# l.h. I II III r.h. C#(17)& F(13) keys		3rd finger	l.h.	
(notation)	Db		3rd finger	l.h.	Addition of low D key (4) to Db fingering may be desirable.
(notation)	D	C# key (7)	thumb	l.h.	
(notation)	D		2nd finger	l.h.	
(notation)	D# r.h. I III		3rd finger	l.h.	Addition of Eb key (19) may be desirable.
(notation)	E l.h. II III r.h. II G (15) key		2nd & 3rd fingers	l.h.	or I II l.h. C# key (7) and trill C# key (7)
(notation)	E		1st finger	l.h.	
(notation)	E l.h. II r.h. G(15)& F(13)keys		1st & 2nd fingers	r.h.	On some bassoons it is better to use l.h. I, instead of l.h. II.
(notation)	F r.h. G (15) & F (13) keys		1st & 2nd fingers	r.h.	
(notation)	F r.h. I II and G (15) key		2nd & 3rd fingers	l.h.	
(notation)	F# with key 10	F# key (10)	thumb	r.h.	Or play F# key(14) and trill key 14.

For this trill	play	trill	with the	of the	Remarks
♪ (notation)	F# with key 14	G# key (11)			Or play F# with key 10 and trill G# key 12
♪ (notation)	G	A♭ key 12 or 11	4th finger or thumb	r.h. r.h.	
♪ (notation)	G	G key (15)	3rd finger	r.h.	
♪ (notation)	G# with key 12 or key 11	G key (15)	3rd finger	r.h.	
♪ (notation)	A♭ with key 12	B♭ key (8)	thumb	r.h.	
♪ (notation)	A	B♭ key (16 or 8)	3rd finger or thumb	r.h.	
♪ (notation)	A		2nd finger	r.h.	
♪ (notation)	B♭ with key 16 or key 8		2nd finger	r.h.	
♪ (notation)	B♭ with key 16 or key 8		1st and 2nd fingers	r.h.	
♪ (notation)	B		1st finger	r.h.	
♪ (notation)	B		3rd finger	l.h.	
♪ (notation)	C	C# key 7 or 17	thumb or 1st finger	l.h. r.h.	
♪ (notation)	C		3rd finger	l.h.	
♪ (notation)	C# l.h. I II III r.h. II G(15) & F(13)		3rd finger	l.h.	
♪ (notation)	D♭ with II G key (15) and F key (13) r.h.		3rd or 1st finger	l.h.	
♪ (notation)	D	G key (15) or C# key (7)	3rd finger or thumb	r.h. l.h.	With 1st trill fingering (key 15) it may be desirable to also trill II r.h.
♪ (notation)	D		2nd finger	l.h.	

For this trill	play	trill	with the	of the	Remarks
	D♯		2nd finger	l.h.	or l.h. I II C♯ key (7) trill: l.h. II
	E♭		1st and 2nd fingers	l.h.	
	E	G key (15)	3rd finger	r.h.	
	E	G key (15) and	2nd finger	r.h.	
	F		2nd finger	r.h.	
	F l.h. II III r.h. I II A♭ key (12)		1st and 2nd fingers	r.h.	or if bassoon has high G trill key, finger F regular way and use trill key.
	F♯	F key (13)	4th finger	r.h.	
	F♯	G key (15)	3rd finger	r.h.	
	G	C♯ and A keys (7 and 6)	thumb	l.h.	Use one half hole I l.h. if necessary.
	G	C♯ and A keys (7 and 6)	thumb	l.h.	At beginning of trill let go right hand I and F key (13).
	G♯	C♯ and A keys (7 and 6)	thumb	l.h.	
	A with low D (4)		3rd finger	l.h.	
	A use F key (13) instead of G key (15)	Trill r.h. II closed and so on l.h. III open alternately			
	B♭		3rd finger	l.h.	
	B		2nd finger	l.h.	
	C		3rd finger	l.h.	On some bassoons trill III r.h. and G key (15) simultaneously.
	C♯		1st finger	l.h.	

Musical Ornamentation (Embellishments)

The following treatment of ornamentation is by no means complete. It is presented here only as a guide to the execution of those ornaments which the student may encounter at this stage of his musical development. There are different manners of performing the same ornament.

The Trill (Shake)

The <u>trill</u> (or shake) consists of the rapid alternation of two tones. They are represented by the printed note (called the principal note) and the next tone above in the diatonic scale. The interval between the two tones may be either a half-step or a whole-step. The signs for the trill are *tr* and ⌁.

An accidental when used in conjunction with the trill sign affects the upper note of the trill.

Be sure to look up each trill fingering in the table.

* The asterisks indicate trill fingerings that differ from fundamental fingerings.

Grace Notes (Appoggiatura)

The grace notes are indicated by notes of a smaller size. They may be divided into two classes, long and short.

Long grace notes

6

WEISSENBORN

Andante sostenuto

7

(1)

In instrumental music of recent composition, the short grace notes should occupy as little time as possible and that value is taken preceding the principal note. They may be single, double, triple or quadruple. The single short grace note is printed as a small eighth note with a stroke through its hook. It is not to be accented. Use trill fingerings when fundamental fingerings are too difficult.

Short grace notes

Patetico — WEISSENBORN

11

Slow waltz time — WEISSENBORN

12

13

14

15

16

The Mordent ᰍ

The short mordent (ᰍ) consists of a single rapid alternation of the principal note with its lower auxiliary. Two or more alternations are executed in the long mordent.

The short inverted mordent (ᰋ) does not have the cross line. In it the lower auxiliary is replaced by the upper. It is the more commonly used mordent in music for the wind instruments.

The mordent takes its value from the principal note.

889-68

In trills of sufficient length a special ending is generally used whether indicated or not

The closing of the trill consists of two tones: the scale tone below the principal note and the principal note.

In long trills of a solo character, it is good taste to commence slowly and gradually increase the speed. Practice the following exercises in the manner of both examples 1 and 2.

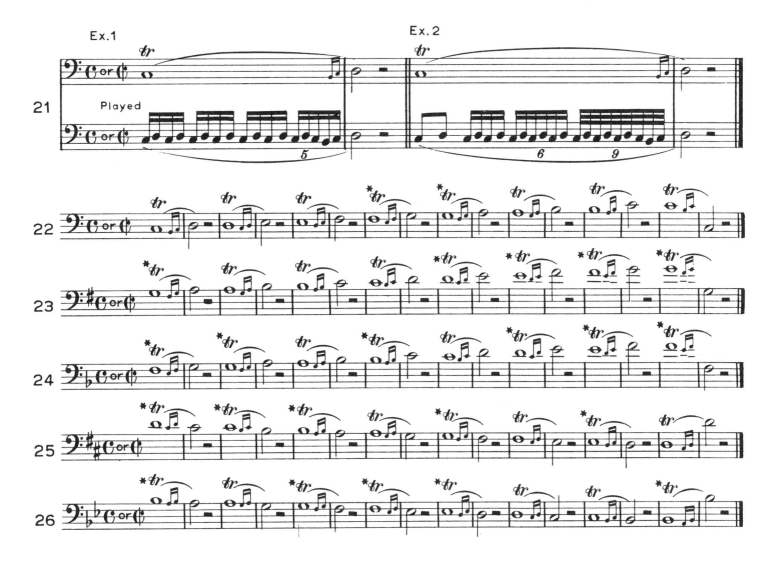

The Turn (Gruppetto)

The turn consists of four tones: the next scale tone above the principal tone, the principal tone itself the tone below the principal tone, and the principal tone again.

When the turn (∞) is placed to the right of the note, the principal note is held almost to its full value, then the turn is played just before the next melody tone. In this case (Ex. 1, 2, 3, 4, and 5) the four tones are of equal length.

When the turn is placed between a dotted note and another note having the same value as the dot (Ex.1 and 3), the turn is then played with the last note of the turn taking the place of the dot, making two notes of the same value. The turn sign after a dotted note will indicate that one melody note lies hidden in the dot.

Sometimes an accidental sign occurs with the turn, and in this case, when written below the sign, it refers to the lowest tone of the turn, but when written above, to the highest (Ex.1 and 2) below.

When the turn is placed over a note (Ex.3) the tones are usually played quickly, and the fourth tone is then held until the time value of the note has expired.

In the inverted turn (Ex.4) the order of tones is reversed, the lowest one coming first, the principal next, the highest third and the principal tone again, last. The inverted turn is indicated by the ordinary turn sign reversed: ∽ or by ⸙ .

Andante

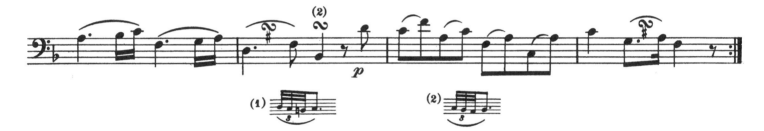

WEISSENBORN

Allegretto moderato

36

SOLOS

O Isis and Osiris
from the Magic Flute

MOZART

German Dance

DITTERSDORF

The Herd Girl's Sunday

Saeterjentens Søndag

OLE BULL

Sarabande

CORELLI

Don't trill eighth note G.

Song Without Words

Bassoon Solo

Bassoon

E. WEISSENBORN, Op. 226
Edited by H. Voxman

889-68

872-1

Romanze

Bassoon Solo

Bassoon

E. WEISSENBORN, Op. 227
Edited by H. Voxman

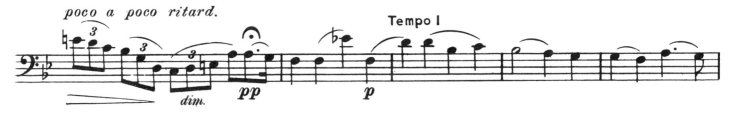